Boneless Ribs

by Hannah Levene

Published by **Lost Alphabet**

With offices at:
1603 Capitol Ave. Cheyenne, WY 82001

United States of America www.lostalphabet.com

ISBN-13: 978-0-9985602-8-1

Library of Congress Cataloging in Publication data available upon request.

Printed in the United States of America

Contents

Dream Sequence 1

The mattress sags.   You take off your top.

I act like you want me to act. Leave my t-shirt on.

Let you pull my jeans off. Hold my breath and puff myself up till I'm tough.

Let you look at the butch parts of me.

You have never sucked my fingers.

You have never stuffed your hand in my mouth.

I have held you round the waist.

I have done what you wanted   better than the boys you said

weren't butch enough.   The mattress sags.

Leave my t shirt on.

Tug at my jeans.

You take off your top.   I have never smelt your underwear.

I keep your number in my top pocket.   I keep your picture

in my wallet, it is soft

like a

licked stamp.

Lay Me in the Back of Your Pick-up Truck and Drive

I am walking slowly home,
trying to drag the world to its knees
in the kind of rebellion which says:
take the weight off your feet.
Like I couldn't radically move.

Lay me in the back of your pick-up truck
and drive. I'll walk slavery slow,
in the kind of rebellion which stretches
its clothes over its head and shows its
irregular and perfect nipples.

Lay me in the up of your truck back pick
and drive. This is the way your tongue moves
when you say *calvin klein.*
This is the way your lips move
when you say *prada.*

Lay me in the pick of your truck up back
and drive. Girls wear swim shorts
butch and beautiful like hockey sticks,
gobbling masculinity attracting bees,
licking their top lips in the sun.

Lay me in the back of your pick-up truck and drive.

A Nest in Wild Love

We were happy then to eat each other only.
Not forever but for
the coming while.
Good that we're so ravenously hungry
that we'll eat again
and however fat we get we fit together.
Worrying,
really,
that we'll never outgrow each other's bodies
even if we outgrow each other's love.

I thought about your cunt so much it seemed like the centre of the world.
Like if someone pulled a plug and everyone swirled somewhere
I'd swirl right into your cunt.
Life felt real and good,
domestic.
Like I was stuffed to brim with plums
and all the stones were massaging my muscles
so I always felt ready,
so I was always limber,
so I could leave at any point.

There was a nest in wild love.
I wondered about your arse,
about arse in general
but I found you perfect, emblazoned on
every surface I looked at for long enough.
Love felt real and good.

PACK

And bright
With lid unlifted yellow.
Wild garlic cradled,
Red ramson,
Coats the roof of our mouths.
Pick me,
Pack my
Lunch at 11
Through boredom,
Through freedom,
Some small cry
For some small help.
New tub holds me.
You won't be hungry
You'll be happy
And bright.

Hot Sandwich Wrapped in Foil

You say: your hair grows and you move and burp
so I know you are alive,
and you are warm and firm like a hot sandwich wrapped in foil.
I can hear you breathing and grinding your teeth
so I know you are alive.
You're so alive! you say,
so I know that I'm alive.

Come on Baby Take a Seat on my Fender

Somewhere in the middle of nowhere
I'm a red flag
red flag limp in the back pocket of your jeans
hip cocked blue jean baby

Tried to slick my hair back
Tried to wear a vest Did

Somewhere in the middle of nowhere I'm a limp red flag
in the back pocket of your jeans
hip cocked blue jean baby

Tried to slick my hair back
kept curling
Tried to feel powerful
kept feeling limp red flag in the back pocket of your blue jeans baby

Somewhere in the middle
of nowhere I'm a red flag
red flag limp in the back pocket of your jeans

Dream Sequence 2: Francois Gilot

You are cracking eggs over Francois Gilot,
reminiscent of the t-shirt you wear to work:
she dries,
reminiscent of the clothes you wore as a child,
skinny,
including ribs and fries
things you weren't born with:
chips in your teeth
and images of Francois Gilot
with yolk drying tightly.

Your body is cool whilst frying bacon
and you wish it was the other way around,
the yolks hardening
on your t-shirt,
drying tightly on your skin,
cracking as you bend your limbs
to crack another egg
over Francois Gilot.

I've Folded the Pages I Think You'll Enjoy

For Elizabeth Bartlett

I've folded the pages I think you'll enjoy,
said goodbye and goodnight to you,

tried to merge feelings
of luckiness and love, but mostly I'm elsewhere,

cutting round the parts I like
and sticking them on my wall.

I'm alive like
the filling of something.

Turning the lights on in the living room when I leave the house
to make it looked lived in.

And you are alive
like yoghurt and bread.

Yes.

I would like a sandwich.
I would like to bite into something and chew.

I'd like something to hold my hands around
and bring to my lips.

I'd like to swallow something
which is more than just the sum of its parts.

We touch stomachs, warm on warm.
We touch bodies red on red.
We love each other more
than just the sum of our parts,

something else from
bread and bread.

In the Morning Girls Filter Out of Rooms in T-Shirts

In the morning girls filter out of rooms in t-shirts
Last night they wore trousers in the morning they don't
Cold green lies about
In the morning
Girls filter out

Then the girls go swimming, dunk into the sea like teabags
Stay still to steep in 'till steeped
Peach parts sunk
Then go swimming
Girls dunk

Eating your Teeth

It will be sweet.
I watch you whilst your dad's talking
about how his dad died
and I think
I'll be there
When you die
and I will be
so fucking sad.
There will be this huge
well of our lives together
to suddenly drown in.
I'll have spent
some of that time
already
worrying that you'll die.
It will be sweet.
Boiled into something suckable 'till
a sharp slither then gone.
Just sugar all over your mouth
you can't feel,
eating your teeth.

Baby I'm Fruit

Baby I'm fruit all alone. Desperate and worried. Freshly dead. Cheeks wet. Eating meat without realising just chomping at the space directly in front of my mouth until it's full.

Mosquitos bite my face in the night, walk all over my body sucking my blood easy as that fruit all alone.

Yeast infected body approached by men.
Ask my name and if I would like to drink coffee or beer.

Sometimes I see girls alone and follow them a little bit.
That's what we have in common and we could talk about that over coffee or beer.

Bite my face in the night, walk all over my body sucking my blood.
Body approached by men.

Cheeks wet eating meat without realising just chomping at our tongues until
someone puts something in our mouths and it's flesh.

Now it's time to bare our tearing teeth. Blood easy. Baby I'm fruit
rotting all alone making booze from my body.

Getting off on the image of me being a drink and it being erotic, feeling erotic when someone uses a straw to drink from me and also when they don't.

Sex like the clink of ice on glass.
Sex like how pubtap coke touches your face before you drink it.
Sex like the booze at the bottom.

How Does It Look?

It looks breath-taking.

Like if you lay in it it'd pound your chest and fill all your holes,

soaked.

All the women stand holding torches draped in concrete,

backs to me, facing

a pool filling more.

And after each song fades, a round of applause,

a standing ovation

roaring like a waterfall,

pounding like it'd pound at your chest

it looks beautiful,

it'd take your breath away.

BONELESS RIBS

I fill myself with blood and try to harden

hold my breath till I bulge
but I'm small

my soft body

I am the minimum amount
of butch you could be:

three pieces of women's clothing.

I slick my hair back,
roll my sleeves up
and try to fill the space with
something.

down on you sings the refrain
down, down, down on you sings the refrain
down, down, down on,
down, down, down on,
down, down, down on you.

butch as boneless ribs sings the refrain *butch as boneless,*
butch as boneless,
butch as boneless ribs.
Butch as boneless,
butch as boneless,
butch as boneless ribs.

Boneless Ribs is a collection of poems about girls loving girls. Challenging the idea of male poet and female muse it asks: how do girls write poems about girls without being boys? You are invited into the poet's dreams of being a body which is strong and tough and shown how this fantasy fails. Instead, the poet offers a definition of the soft-butch identity as boneless ribs. This dish of boneless bones reminding us of our detachment from the bodies we consume and desire. The book is a conversation between the visceral and the imaginary; somewhere between a collection of poetry and a collection of dirty dreams.

Hannah Levene is a writer living in the U.K.
Her poetry collection Boneless Ribs follows years of hosting poetry nights and self-publishing poetry pamphlets.

Lost Alphabet

12977523R00015

Printed in Great Britain
by Amazon